EASY NETWORK MARKETING

"DO WHATEVER THE HEART WANTS ,ONE DAY WILL BE SUCCESS" BY-- JOT CHAHAL

I0483090

JOT CHAHAL

ISBN 978-1-64650-359-9

This book has been published with all efforts taken to make the material error-free after the consent of the author. However, the author and the publisher do not assume and hereby disclaim any liability to any party for any loss, damage, or disruption caused by errors or omissions, whether such errors or omissions result from negligence, accident, or any other cause.

While every effort has been made to avoid any mistake or omission, this publication is being sold on the condition and understanding that neither the author nor the publishers or printers would be liable in any manner to any person by reason of any mistake or omission in this publication or for any action taken or omitted to be taken or advice rendered or accepted on the basis of this work. For any defect in printing or binding the publishers will be liable only to replace the defective copy by another copy of this work then available.

Contents

Preface

The purpose of writing this network marketing book is to tell you all about network marketing well and how profitable it can be. Every word has been written with hard work and dedication.

Easy Network Marketing will help people to begin Network Marketing in a simple manner. It will allow you to eliminate unnecessary mistakes and save time. Additionally, you will be able to tackle your team better. In turn,you will learn more in less time.

Ultimately, you will learn how to Build a solid career in Network Marketing and Create Unlimited Leads. During the process, you will learn simple practical format, use social media for prospecting as a pre - invite technique and Understand the art of inviting and appointment setting. Through this,you will learn to Edification rules and tips and Understand and counter non stated objections in prospect's mind. You will be able to Show your business plan as per technique acceptable to human mind. You will learn Practical closing techniques for Network Marketing, in addition to Follow up rules and tips. You will learn about Personality development for a perfect Networker. The book also explains how to Understand body language for rapport building and Personal Branding tips to kick start your marketing campaign. To do this,you will Learn the art of duplication etc.

I am positive that this book will be helpful in your quest of network managing

Acknowledgements

To begin, I would like to thank the Almighty for giving me the intellect to create this book.

I would like to thank my Mother and Father for always supporting me in everything I do. Words are not enough to explain how thankful i am to those who have joined me on this journey.

While learning about network Marketing, I felt there were not enough modern guides available to the public. This guide is easily accessible and user friendly. I hope it helps you on your quest of network marketing,and wish you all the best

Ranjot Singh
Ebook Publisher: Rana Books India
Paperback Publisher : NotionPress

About Author

Ranjot Singh

Ranjot Singh, also known as the name Jot Chahal, has wrote many books which he has recently published. As well as writing, Chahal is also a Third-Year student in BCA (Degree name)from Punjabi University Patiala Baba Jogi Peer Neighbourhood Campus, Ralla He belongs to Mansa district of Punjab. His books contains many poetry and quotes which reflects his thoughts and touches the reader's heart. His most recent book, The Perfect Life (100+ Positive thoughts for your life): Everything in your hands. His books are mainly in English, Hindi and Punjabi.

CHAPTER ONE

Introduction

Introduction to Network Marketing for Online Marketers

A lot of people have radical views one way or the other about Network marketing, also known as Multi-Level Marketing (MLM). For some, it's one of the best opportunities for entry level entrepreneurs to own their own business with very little investment. For others, it's some sort of shady or sinister endeavor that should be avoided at all costs.The truth is that MLM is a legitimate business model that has been used successfully by some of the biggest and most successful companies in the US, including Amway, PrePaid Legal, Exel, Meleleuca and USANA.

Who Is Involved with Network Marketing?

Most of the people in the network marketing industry are honest, hardworking individuals who are simply trying to earn a living to provide a high quality lifestyle for themselves and their families. Sadly, like any industry, network marketing also includes a small number of dishonest people who poison the well for everybody else so that the entire concept of MLM is seen in a dim light by people ignorant of the facts.

In this article, we are going to look at the advantages network marketing offers to both experienced entrepreneurs and to those just starting out. We also will look at the opportunities it presents for honest people who are willing to work hard running their own business. Don't worry, we're not going to try to sell you any cleaning products or timeshares!

Definition of Network Marketing

Network marketing is a marketing strategy in which the people are paid not only for sales they generate themselves, but also for the sales of other salesmen they recruit. This business model is known as a "downline model" because it has distributors and a hierarchy that involves multiple levels of compensation.

It's different than single-level marketing., which is when salesmen are compensated for products they sell directly consumers.

Network Marketing Structure

In network marketing business, the sales force pays a portion of their revenues to the person who recruited them. That person then pays a portion of all of their revenues to the person on the level above them, and so on. This is what is known as an "upline revenue structure".

The first network marketing platforms were launched in the 1950's and involved nutritional supplements, household products, and cosmetics. By the 1980s, MLM businesses had grown to include companies specializing in insurance and long-distance telephone services.

By the 21st Century, technological advances enabled network marketing to expand into credit cards, travel, pre-paid legal services and other successful areas.

There are all types of network marketing platforms. And in many cases people can get into the market for very little upfront investment while still enjoying the benefits of owning their own business. MLM opportunities usually are far less costly than buying a business franchise.

In most network marketing platforms, salespeople sell products directly to consumers by means of relationship referrals and word of mouth marketing.

Common Network Marketing Misconceptions

Let's address some of the most common misconceptions about network marketing. A lot of people have a bad opinion of network marketing because occasionally it attracts people looking to exploit its structure to reap financial reward with very little work. In other words, people who simply want to "get rich quick".

Network marketing is also criticized because the upline revenue stream is structured like a pyramid. This creates confusion among people who think all network marketing must be a "pyramid scheme" or a "Ponzi scheme".

These toxic terms refer to illegal business models in which people on the bottom of the pyramid invest in business opportunities but get little or no return on their investment. The people at the top of the pyramid keep most or all the money and don't deliver the goods or services they promised.

The reality is that network marketing is simply a non-traditional business model. It's more like "microfranchising" than anything else. MLM can be a good choice for people because it has a very low cost of entry and there is the potential to earn a lot of money.

Is Network Marketing a Risky Business?

Some people make money in network marketing businesses and some people lose money. But the same can be said for traditional business models such as franchising. The success or failure of the individual under either scenario has less to do with the structure of the business model itself than it does with the person's understanding of their market, the effort they made to create opportunities for themselves, and even just plain luck.

Most network marketing businesses focus on creating opportunities for people who might otherwise not have them, including people who:

- Lack experience running their own business
- Have little previous sales experience
- Are unhappy with their current income level
- Have been unsuccessful running previous businesses

Network marketing businesses offer these people the opportunity to be achieve high levels of success. But, if it's not your thing, there are other ways to make money online, such as promoting affiliate offers (like ours).

Advantages & Disadvantages

1. The first and foremost advantage of it is that company saves a lot of costs due to networking marketing because marketing is done through individuals which is less expensive as compared to traditional method of advertising like television, online medium, newspaper and so on.

2. As far as individuals are concerned they also benefit from this marketing because they get the opportunity to work from home and be their own boss. Hence individuals who have the strong network of friends and family can make a lot of money by just selling or marketing the product to their network. Hence in a way this marketing helps the individuals to become entrepreneurs without too much investment as this type of marketing requires strong network rather than capital or money.

3. Another benefit of it is that it does not require any professional degree or experience like MBA to start network marketing and hence it gives the opportunity to all types of people whether they are pensioners or students or housewives and even working people can start it on part time basis. Hence in a way network marketing gives flexibility to people thinking of earning extra income without doing too much effort.

Disadvantages of Network Marketing

1. The biggest disadvantage of this type of marketing is that majority of companies and schemes are fraud and it is very difficult to trust on such schemes and companies which in turn make the task of genuine companies also difficult as individuals treat every company as fraud and therefore they will not market the products of the companies easily to their networks.

2. Another disadvantage of it is that individuals who do network marketing are amateur and not professionals and that results in even good products being marketed badly resulting in overall bad impression about the company and in case of marketing 1 dissatisfied customer will lead to company losing 10 customers and hence in a way network marketing can create more bad image than good image due to lack of experience and expertise of individuals doing network marketing.

3. Another limitation of it is that people believe what they see and since in the case of network marketing there is no use of marketing channels like television, newspapers and internet people are uncomfortable with products which are sold through network marketing as they have never seen the products before. Hence in simple words, lack of awareness about the products make this type of marketing a tough job for the companies doing this marketing.

As one can see from the above that network marketing has advantages as well as disadvantages and any individual thinking of doing it should first check the authenticity of company as there is no easy way of earning money and those network marketing which promises to get rich quickly are scam, hence one should be careful while doing this type of marketing.

CHAPTER TWO

Common Criticisms

Now with that being said, let me get into a few things when you think about network marketing that gives network marketing a bad rep.

People that Join Everything

One is when people join everything. It's extremely annoying. No one likes it. You lose friends, because every day you want to sell a new product. Just so you know, people get tired of it.

I experienced this when I was 20 years old. There was a period of time when my friends said, "I don't want to have anything to do with this." That's why I said that I would never touch anything again that has anything to do with network marketing.

But there are a lot of people that want to join anything and everything. They tell people, "Hey, you should join this! I found this new thing!" It's too much. It's like you're prostituting products. There's a lot of that in network marketing and that's a turn off.

Something New to Sell Every Single Month

The second one is when they have something new to sell every single month. This is similar to the other one that I told you about. One month they're selling you some travel product. The next month it's a Tahitian Noni that's going to change your life. The next day it's a water that if you drink it will make you younger. Every day there's something new to sell.

Inventory in Garage

Third, inventory in the garage. This is very problematic. Here's why. People end up with inventory in the garage when they've been oversold a product that they can't afford and shouldn't buy. Don't tell people, "Hey, come buy $5,000 worth of products."

Why are you doing that? The person doesn't need it and if they don't have a track record of selling a lot of products, they shouldn't do it.

People need to like and use the product and if they want to buy more products, you can show them other elements of the product. Otherwise people spend $5,000 on products that they end up selling on eBay for $600. That's a rip off, and you shouldn't do that to people.

Get Rich Quick Message

Next is get rich quick. This is one that's very annoying to most people. It's the idea that you'll be a millionaire in no time. People don't like that. It's deceptive and it's not something you ought to be doing.

Misrepresentation

Misrepresentation is when you say things like, "This is the cure to cancer" or claim to cure aging, make people happy, improve your sex life, and give you more energy.

Misrepresentation happens way too much in the world of network marketing and it gives a bad rep.

More Focus on Compensation Plan Than on the Product

Here's the other one that's very concerning. When a guy comes up to you and sells you the company like this, "Hey, who cares what the product is? We have the best compensation plan." Listen. Run away as far as possible. When they sell compensation plan first, product second, I have a problem. When they sell compensation plan first and product second, we have a very, very big problem. It's got to be product first, then compensation plan. You first got to buy into the product.

But there are a lot of people that sell compensation plan first. As a matter of fact, you'll see a lot of videos and you'll see a lot of people present and they'll say, "We have this. . . " and you still don't know what the product is. "Here's how much money was made with this." No, no, no. It's not a good approach and it gives the industry a bad rep.

Too Many Fake Scripts

Next, too many fake scripts. Look, I remember one of the reasons why I didn't like going to church, one of the reasons why I was an Atheist for 25 years. Let me tell you why I was an Atheist for 25 years. I was an Atheist and an agnostic, it would always change. And I wouldn't like going to church. Here's why. People had the best scripts in the world. "Oh praise the Lord, my brother! God bless you! You know John 3:16? Oh my gosh!" And I remember this one guy one time pulled me aside and he says, there's nothing more annoying than a Christian man who's learned the script but never lives it themselves.

And in the world of business and especially network marketing, there are people that know the script. It sounds the same, but there's no results and nothing going on. It's too scripted without anything really happening in their lives. It's very obvious and people can read it.

No Real Product

Next, red flags to pay attention to. You know I already told you about no real product. So there was a company called ZeekRewards. And I remember one guy came and met with me at Maggiano's. Very, very smart guy. He was a very open guy. Here's what he told me about ZekeRewards. He said, "Pat, I know this company's not going to last for another two years. But we can do this and maybe we can make a million dollars in the next six, 12 months." I don't have the desire to do anything like that.

They ended up going out of business, but not only going out of business; they owner owes people I think $600 million, the attorney general shut them down. If you go online and type them up you'll see it. It's companies like that that give bad rep to all these industries. I mean, people like that don't need to be in the business world, right?

Not effective. Not effective. So you've got to make sure there's a real product.

Only Make Money From Recruiting

And then last but not least, is the obvious one. If you just make money from recruiting, that's the pyramid scheme. There was a company back in the day, it was called 2x2.net and what it did was it allowed you to buy seven spots. Let me tell you what seven spots is. You literally would buy your own position, then you would buy two other positions and you would buy two other positions and it was $420 per position. I never got involved, but I studied it. I had to find out exactly what was going on in the marketplace. So one position. . . $2800. The Attorney General came. . . guys were rolling in Lamborghinis. Every single place you saw, there was a Lamborghini. Green Lamborghini, purple Lamborghini. Everywhere you saw Lamborghinis, with 2x2.net sticker on the side.

They eventually went out of business. Why? Because you can't just buy multiple spots. That is not the real way of doing business. And their only product was a portal, and that's not how the money was being made. Eventually it got shut down. There's got to be real, tangible product, and you cannot make money from just recruiting people, when they pay $420 and make 200 bucks, that cannot happen if there's not a real product that's taking place.

Consumer benifited

Almost every human is already in network marketing but not all get paid for their recommendation as most of them do it without realising it (& being officially recognised by the company). Network marketing is as the name suggests- it's marketing of products & services within the network. Here the network implies - your circle of influence. It works on a simple principal of a consumer is using & sharing it's experience about the products & services of any company. E.g. You came to know about Quora through someone already using it & that person recommended it to you. And I'm sure you also must have recommended it within your network. So technically you did what people working with network marketing company do, you do didn't get paid for it by Quora as it doesn't recognise you as official promoter of their platform. But your recommendation has benefited them in increasing the user base that every company is looking for increase. Don't be surprised if sometime in future you get the news of Quora being acquired by some other company for huge valuation. And this valuation is due to its user base like Whatsapp. Just imagine how much cost effective & productive this 'network marketing' is for companies and that's why many companies in the world are moving to this business platform.

By now I'm sure you must have understood that you're also promoting products & services of different companies but not getting anything in return for increasing their turn over / revenue.

It is this very reason everyone should get into 'Network Marketing' industry with right company so that you also get paid for your efforts

CHAPTER THREE

People to Talk

1. Have a party and invite friends and family

Although some people are not comfortable asking their friends and family to join their MLM opportunity, they can be a great way to get your business off of the ground. This doesn't mean that you have to harass your own mother until she gives in, but you can definitely use your relationships to get started. You should have a casual gathering where you invite some friends and family that you think might be interested in a business opportunity and then go from there.

2. Use social media

Twitter and Facebook are easy and free ways to quickly get your message to a large group of people. However, you should avoid spamming and other annoying practices that turn people away. Instead, you should use your Facebook page as a way to interact with people. Give them a reason to come to your page, such as a special offer or coupon code. Make Tweets and updates sparingly and make sure they contain useful information that piques people's interest.

3. Identify your target market

Your target market is the demographic that is most likely to buy your product or want to join you MLM business. You should identify who this target market is and then develop the best strategies to reach them. This could mean posting your link on blog sites in a similar niche or even buying PPC advertising from a search engine. This is a great way to get people that are interested to listen to your pitch.

4. Go to events

A great way to get exposure for your MLM opportunity is by attending MLM events or trade shows related to your product or service. This will allow you to get in front of other people in the industry, or people that are interested in your type of product or service. One large trade show could get you massive exposure.

5. Be passionate!

This is probably the most important thing, as you will not be able to sell your idea to other people unless you are passionate about it yourself. People can sense when someone truly believes in a product or service they are selling and this passion is attractive. When you are talking to people about your MLM opportunity you need to show that you truly believe in what you are saying. This will give them the trust necessary to take the next step and join your team.

Marketing Ideas

1. Promote your social media handles, even in person
2. Join in on popular hash tags
3. Create short, engaging Vine videos
4. Pin your site images and graphics on Pinterest
5. Keep tabs on competitors' social profiles
6. Try urban marketing like flyers, posters, and sidewalk chalk
7. Commission a mural
8. Use your surroundings to your advantage
9. Consider unusual sponsorships
10. Host a photo contest
11. Host a video contest
12. Host a voting contest
13. Host a caption contest
14. Host a good old-fashioned sweepstakes
15. Post to deal sites like Group on
16. Add a hash tag to your contests
17. Make contests super sharable on social media
18. Offer bonus points for sharing contests
19. Notify email subscribers of contests
20. Promote your contest on (all) social media
21. Write content catered to your audience
22. Add a visual element to ALL your content pieces
23. Create data-packed info graphics
24. Use templates to make content creation easier
25. Include graphs and charts in your content
26. Use videos for interactivity
27. Leverage the power of lists

28. Make bold future predictions

29. Inject controversy into your copy

30. Aggregate awesome content from other sources

31. Create an "ask the experts" roundup

32. Write relevant top 10 lists

33. And other lists, too!

34. Write a product comparison guide

35. Link to your existing content with CTAs

36. Post presentations on Slideshare

37. Host free webinars

38. Get ideas from Google related search

39. Use pop-up opt-ins on landing pages

40. Use analytics to take advantage of popular content

41. Write eBooks

42. Create 101 guides to teach the basics

43. Promote your content

44. Post about industry hot topics

45. Write (and allow) guest posts

46. Create white papers

47. Only generate quality content

48. Give your company some personality and don't be afraid to use it

49. Contribute to online magazines

50. Host a podcast

CHAPTER FOUR

Grow Your Network

STEP #1 – BE PROUD OF THE EFFORT YOU HAVE PUT IN

Misrepresenting the facts is really hurting Network Marketing.

When a person is so focused on signing up a new recruit that they are willing to minimize the effort, skill, and time it takes to build a successful Network Marketing business, they are hurting the profession as a whole. Further, you are creating an illusion that is not real, and will more often than not result in fast distributor dropout when they realize it requires actual work.

My advice is, be 100% honest. Tell your prospects how much effort it has taken. Tell them the steps you took. Tell them the skills you had to learn. Do NOT tell them that it practically grows itself and it is so easy anyone can become a millionaire in three weeks. Misrepresenting the facts will only lead to failure in the future.

Our stories are what relate to other people. When you tell your story to a prospect, they will think one of two things. First, they may think, "There is no way I could go through all that." Second, they may think, "I am up for the challenge, let's do this!"

Being honest with your prospect from the beginning will automatically weed out the people who do not have what it takes. It will save you time, money and effort down the road.

STEP #2 – INVEST IN YOUR FUTURE

There is almost no career on this planet that does not require training. As Network Marketers we have to learn a ton of skills. You have to wear so many different hats that at times it helps just to list them out.

- **Marketing Guru**
- **Communication Expert**
- **Product Expert**
- **Motivational Coach**
- **Time Management Wizard**
- **Recruiting Agent**
- **Team Leader**

The list goes on and on but the need to learn something new every single day does not change. I encourage you to take time each day and advance your skills in each of these areas. Then when you recruit someone new make sure you convey your routine. It will not only prepare that recruit for what lies ahead, but it will make you the authority on how to succeed in Network Marketing.

STEP #3 – FOCUS ON THE LIVES OF YOUR TEAM

Defining why you are a Network Marketer is an important task. The easy answer is, to make a living. However, we are afforded a greater opportunity in this profession. We have the ability to improve and provide for people far beyond our immediate reach.

How many people do you know that could use a second stream of income?

How many families do you know that barely make it by?

If you take the time to define your purpose and if you decide that improving the lives of the people that you come in contact with, then Network Marketing can do so much more than provide you with income.

Common Mistakes to Avoid

1. Lack of Team Spirit

If you lack team spirit, how do you expect to succeed in this industry? The very core of network marketing is to network amongst your team while working cohesively towards the same vision.

Network Marketing is the act of bringing together a group of people for a mutual benefit. It generally answers the question "How can I help?" rather than "What can you do for me?"!

Having a team that you communicate with regularly helps you gain new and fresh ideas about the business and holds you accountable to staying plugged in with the daily activities that will get you closer to your goals.

By communicating with your organization, you're not only creating the opportunity to inspire your own team; you're also developing meaningful and valuable relationships with them.

To avoid this common mistake, conduct a weekly group meeting with your team and use this time to assess each other's performance, provide feedback, give suggestions, and share insights in improving your group's overall productivity.

2. Misleading prospects into attending a business opportunity meeting

Unfortunately, there are an increasing number of network marketers who exercise this technique to gain prospective leads. They invite friends over for a seemingly weekend bonding, only to take them to an opportunity meeting without telling them so. What's worse, their prospects show no interest at all for the business.

"Kidnapping" your potential partners is not the way to go. You are not just wasting their time, you are also wasting yours. Invite prospects that are already aware of your intentions and have expressed interest beforehand.

To avoid this common and deceptive practice, be very clear with your intentions and follow your companies system to inviting your prospects to a meeting.

3. Lack of Focus in the Industry

Most people are switching from one company to another in hopes of landing that one business that will make them rich instantly. Instead of focusing on a single company, they chose to diversify and put all their resources to waste by diverting their attention multiple different ways.

If you really want to avoid this common practice, I'd suggest focusing on one company that you firmly believe will be the gateway to your success, and give it 100% of your time, energy and effort.

Most businesses take 2-3 years to build successfully, so make a time commitment to give it all you got during that time. If for any reason, you see that you're giving 100% but changes or flaws in the company have altered your vision for reaching your goals, only then should you begin considering changing over to a new company, where you can be 100% focused again.

Success requires F.O.C.U.S., which simply means Follow One Course Until Successful. If you know you've been jumping around without clear focus, then now's the time to intentionally change this bad habit.

4. Disregarding Personal Development

Personal Development is the first step that you must invest in to accomplish success in building your mind-set. Although you will be given tons of training, tools and mentors, your success relies in your ability to have the right mind-set.

Personal Development is a highly encouraged practice that is enforced on every individual who joins the industry. From the team meetings, to business presentations, you'll find that Personal Development is the foundation for which nearly all Network Marketing companies are built.

If you disregard and overlook this common practice, expect downfall to follow. If you haven't enforced it on yourself, then this might be the reason why you're not thriving on success.

In order for you to move forward, you have to learn the key elements of personal development: mind-set, technical knowledge, and leadership. Keep in mind, personal development is a continuous process. It doesn't end in the four corners of schools and universities that you've attended. So spend a great deal of your time constantly feeding yourself with positive reinforcement and surround yourself with successful and motivated people.

5. *Easily swayed to rejection and negative outside influence*

Do you know that our warm market can be our worst enemy? Before we proceed to the cold market, it is common practice to share what we know and what we have with the people closest to us, which is generally family and old friends.

Experiencing rejection directly from the very people whom we least expect can be very hard to accept. Not only does it kill the enthusiasm, the negative reaction can also create self-doubt—especially for beginners.

You may not control what other people will tell you or how they will react, but you can control your response to it. Prepare for them by equipping yourself with optimistic viewpoints all the time, and educate yourself on the multiple ways to deal with rejection.

Remember, no one can steal your dreams and enthusiasm from you unless you let them.

CHAPTER FIVE

Reasons of importance

1.An Opportunity To Earn Extra Cash

Every human being has a desire to make extra cash and achieve financial freedom. Network marketing offers you an opportunity to generate income despite your current financial standing. With network marketing, you do not need to quit your day job as you can do network marketing as a side hustle.

2.Residual Income

Residual income is an earning that you continue to receive based on your earlier efforts. Residual income is based on sales of products and services. This means that, if your network continues to generate repeat sales, then you will get paid for that one sale long into the future. Network marketing is important because it enables you to earn more and work less by building your passive income sources.

3.Huge Demand For Excellent Products

Network marketing companies are famous for creating revolutionary products that hit the market by storm. The huge demand for these products makes it easier to sell. Also, the products are designed specifically to generate repeat business. Network marketing has enabled brands to grow into multi-billion companies through endless chains of agents who ensure that the multiple levels keep growing and advancing progressively.

4.Live A Rewarding Life

One important reason that makes network marketing important is the personal development that comes from helping other people succeed. It is very rewarding to lift other people and watch them become better every day. With network marketing, you grow as your business grows. Your skills, strengths, and experiences are also rewarded with handsome pay-outs which are very important for both part-time and full-time business distributors.

5.Leveraging

Leveraging is a magnificent tool for building wealth. In network marketing, building your network and watching it grow is of paramount importance. Multi-level marketing helps customers find what they need. When you and your team work together by developing a collective mind-set, the business begins to build itself. You start enjoying the benefits of network marketing. For example, you can go for a vacation and make money while at it. When you teach others how to do business you reap the rewards as well, creating win-win relationships.

Important Skills

1. Connecting and Booking Meetings

The first skill to learn is making connections with people. This is the marketing part. This can be done in many different ways like talking with friends and family, or connecting with people who are not in your immediate network. This can be face to face or over the telephone and at first will probably make you feel uncomfortable. This is normal and just remember it gets easier and easier over time. The goal is to set a time where you can show people the business presentation and let them decide if it is a good fit for them or not.

2. Presenting The Opportunity

The next skill to master is the ability of sharing the business opportunity. This varies from company to company but is normally done through a 20 minute business presentation. Most people are not used to giving presentations in front of people and again, this will likely make you feel uncomfortable at first. This too gets easier over time, until you wonder how it ever scared you. Just remember, you are showing people a way to massively improve their lives.

3. Following Up

Remember this saying, "the fortune is in the follow up". It's a fact that most people don't join straight away. This is because it takes on average 7-10 touch points, from people first hearing about it, to feeling comfortable for getting started. This is business. This means you are going to have to get used to keeping in regular contact with people and progressing them along the stages. This takes practice, patience and organisation. Most people don't get going straight away and thats alright.

4. Sponsoring and Launching

The next skill set to develop is being able to launch your new business partner and get them going and growing in the fastest time possible. It is normal for people to experience fear when first starting out as they have just taken a leap of faith. We all go through this. To help get the maximum momentum, you have to get in front of your new consultants network asap. It is the fastest way to grow both your businesses. But say it with me...it gets easier and easier the more you do it.

5. Training and Coaching

Once you have a new consultant it is time to teach them what you know. This is all about taking them through basic training and helping them overcome obstacles and become successful. You are now their "Business Coach" helping them through their problems and keeping them on the track to success. It is very rewarding watching people develop and grow in to people they always knew they could become.

6. Goals, Planning and Time Management

Setting goals, planning and time management is a crucial skill set in business which needs learning, practicing, developing and mastering. Like with all the other skill sets, this is something that we do not learn in school. It is something we have to learn and continually work on each day, week, month and year, until it becomes a habit. The good news is that after 3 months practice, when it is a new habit, it becomes just as easy as brushing your teeth in the morning.

7. Personal Development

Personal development is another critical factor in success. Remember This: Network marketing is not hard or easy. It is what it is. The problem, is that when you first start out it is you that is not very good. You have to work on yourself to get better. You have to work on your habits (bad habits). You have to work on your skills and beliefs. Don't wish things were easier, wish that you were better. The better you get, the easier it all becomes.

CHAPTER SIX

Get More Customers

1. Set a time budget each week or month for your networking. Plan to attend a specific number of meetings or events at which you can network. Make sure your other tasks and responsibilities fit around these meetings. It's best to balance networking with your other lead generating activities. This way you can measure the value of your networking leads against the time spent acquiring them.

2. Pick networking opportunities that put you face to face with people most likely to need what you offer. Or try to meet people who can connect you with people who need what you offer. Both are good prospects.

3. Understand why you're there - to begin relationships - not to sell. Networking is the first step in a long dance. Don't rush.

4. Don't give your cards to everyone. Save your money and some trees. Hand out your card only to people who ask for it.

5. Ask people questions. Learn about them and their business. This is how you pre-qualify them. If they meet your target criteria ask for their card. If not, don't.

6. Don't sell yourself. It's okay to tell people what you do. Give your "30 second commercial" but stop after that. You're there to gather information and to meet people, not to sell.

7. People love people who are interested in them. Ask questions, listen and engage people. This is the fastest way to develop rapport with someone. It's also the best way to determine quickly if they're someone you should be doing business with.

8. Have fun, relax and enjoy yourself. People like being around people who are relaxed and having fun.

9. Don't corner people and don't get cornered. Manage your time and conversation so you can meet enough people to justify your time spent networking.

10. Offer referrals. The best way to begin a relationship is by giving someone something - like a referral. It doesn't cost you anything. If they're the kind of person you want to do business with, they'll reciprocate and a valuable, long-tem business relationship could develop.

Networking is a time-honoured way of developing business relationships. It can be done in networking groups or clubs. It can be done through Chambers of Commerce. It can be done anywhere you meet people. If you are active in your community or industry, you can easily network. Some people "network" while shopping for groceries!

It all depends on your attitude and your focus. The more people you meet who might need your product or service, the more potential customers you can have

Various Ways of Marketing

Direct Marketing

Direct marketing is for me to sell my product by going directly to the consumer, or going directly to the business. With direct marketing, I have a product; let me show it to you. Will you buy it? If yes, you pay me and in exchange for money, I give you the product, and I make a profit off the sale.

Email Marketing

Next you have email marketing. For many years people that did email marketing were called the biggest con artists because they would say things like, "This is an elite thing that only seven people will be a part of, and you have an opportunity to be part of the seven." And people would respond, "Oh my gosh, I've got to be part of it." A lot of people called people that did this con artists, but there's a creative part to it and it can be very effective.

Telemarketing

Some do telemarketing. Telemarketing is a philosophy of marketing where people in a call center make sales calls and some people buy. It's effective for some people because if you throw enough against the wall, some of it sticks.

Affiliate Marketing

Another one is affiliate marketing. What's affiliate marketing? Affiliate marketing is hey, let us put this on your website. If somebody clicks on it, we'll give you $3. If somebody buys the product, we'll give you $25."

Network Marketing

Another one is network marketing. What is network marketing? I am marketing my product to who? To my network. That's all it is. I am marketing my product to my network. That's network marketing.

Multilevel Marketing

An example of network marketing is when back in the day, ING Direct said, "If you help someone else open up an ING Direct account, we'll give you $25."

But, multi-level marketing says the following. "If you find somebody else who refers ING and they open up an account, we'll pay him $25, and we'll pay you $5." Now it becomes a level. So it's multilevel. We'll pay two generations, that's where the level comes in.

Guerrilla Marketing

Then you have guerrilla marketing. An example of guerrilla marketing is when you had guys that came out with a CD and they marketed it in the streets, just hitting a ton of people at the same time. Some call this a very con and deceptive way of doing it, but it's effective. And many major hip hop people and movie people in the world that you respect started with guerrilla marketing.

Behavioral Marketing

Next is behavioral marketing. Sometimes people say, "Hey, the weirdest thing happened today. I went on this website just two days ago to buy furniture, and today every website I go to is advertising the same furniture to me. There's something weird going on." No, it's called behavioural marketing. Some people feel this is a little deceptive, but it's just marketing! And people buy the product because they simply see your fingerprints of where you went on the web and they advertise accordingly.

Digital Marketing

Next is digital marketing. What's digital marketing? Social media. It's very, very effective. Now some people say, "I'm sick and tired of seeing ads on social media. Every time I watch a video, this guy keeps coming up." But this is digital marketing and it works.

Celebrity Marketing

Celebrity Marketing is when a celebrity or athlete says, "Hey, I used this product and it changed my life!" MJ Hanes, LeBron, and Shaq are examples.

Cross Marketing

Then you have cross marketing. Cross marketing is when, for example, a real estate agent teams up with accountants. It's when you team up with someone and cross market products.

Trade Show Marketing

Next, trade show marketing. Trade shows are all some people talk about. And others say, "I would never do a trade show. It's so annoying." But there are many successful trade show marketers.

T.V. Marketing

Then you have T.V. marketing. A lot of people do T.V. advertisement. It's some of the most manipulative marketing tactics. You know why? It gives people the impressions such as, "If you drink this beer you're going to get laid." Or, "Take this pill and your erections may last for the rest of your life!" People watching that may say, "Oh my gosh! Give me one of those pills! I want an erection that lasts a lifetime." Give me a break! This is manipulative, but it works.

Radio

And then you have radio. Nowadays I think there are only three people that listen to the radio. I think the best people in radio marketing are those that sell radio. In 2009, 2010, I spent $100,000 on radio and it didn't work. Radio's not what it used to be, but some people still do radio marketing.

CHAPTER SEVEN

"Magic" words

1. Ruthlessness

This is a strange word, but the correct one, I believe. It signifies how you must protect and manage your time and attention. Everyone has the same 24 hours in a day, but you cannot afford to waste a single one. These are your most valuable resources. Cut out distractions.

Allocate time for your family and your main obligations. Give your employer the time to which you have agreed. Be on time for work so that you can leave work on time. By leaving work on time you can make appointments to call clients, downline, and still have time for your family. Be jealous of everything you do everyday and ask yourself, "Is this consistent with my family and business priorities and goals?".

2. Congruency

If you do not believe in what you are selling, 100%, you are a liar. It doesn't matter if you are selling cars, insurance, water filters, pills, potions, lotions, or silly putty. If you do this you are lying to your customer, your sponsor, you are lying to your spouse, you are lying to your downline, and worst of all, you are lying to yourself.

To be in congruence means to be in harmony with everything you are doing. It's a crime against yourself and your family to sell something in which you do not have full confidence. Your thoughts and your actions must be in accord. Now this is separate from possibly being lied to by the company or officials of the company.

If, given the information at your disposal, you believe in what you are selling, then you are congruent with your actions and therefore are on track for success.

3. Willingness

Are you willing to do what it takes. Some things are fun and many are not fun. All of these tasks are necessary to your success. Follow-up tasks may not always be fun, but as the network marketing cliche goes, "The fortune is in the Follow-up".

Olympic skaters and swimmers who are in the gym at 4:00AM doing the things that others will not so they can have the things that others will not is the purest model. You have to be willing to help, to talk, to do just that much extra. This is a universal to true walk-away residual income success in network marketing.

That kind of success is made of many factors company, compensation, product and market but to a person these ultra-successful entrepreneurs will say that have always been willing to go the extra mile. Now it's your turn. Are you that good?

4. Foolishness

You must be willing to take risks and to seem foolish. You have to take a chance on your 1st or 2nd or 13th presentation being the one of which you are proud. Are you willing to be on stage, in front of 1 person or 20, and say things that may be incorrect?

Remember the old networking chestnut "Ignorance on fire is better than Knowledge on ice" well, I certainly believe that being in motion is more important than having every answer correct. You just have to continue to work on that ignorance even while you are in motion and not use that ignorance or the embarrassment it can cause as an excuse to do nothing. Action is critical.

You must be in motion, somewhat in control, and learning from your mistakes constantly. Be involved constantly on the edge of your competence. You must stretch and learn constantly. Be a fool or do not. Choose.

5. Vigilance

You should constantly be looking for new opportunities. Search the news for articles regarding your marketplace or your company's competitors. Look for new markets and ways of reaching those markets. Use the Internet, Google News Alerts(tm), and any resources you can develop.

Talk to local governmental agencies which oversee your marketplace for new marketing ideas. Do not sit and wait for your company or your upline to open new avenues of marketing or product lines, engage your whole mind. If you want to be successful it might, just might, take all of you. Twenty percent or 75 percent of you may just not be enough. Leave nothing to chance.

AMAZING BENEFITS

1. Low Start Up Costs

You can start a network marketing business with either very little investment or no investment at all. In most cases, your initial investment you are required to pay as start-up capital will not even come close to your earning potential - which, if taken seriously will pay out much more compared to other types of businesses. The best thing about investing in this type of business is that there are very minimum monthly costs such as your monthly auto-ship that can cost anywhere from $50 - $100/month with products you consume. What's great is that the operating systems are already in place for you such as a back-office, sales/financial tracker, marketing material, replicated website, corporate training, etc. which some companies charge a monthly fee for. Basically, you're getting a business that is already built, market research and costs of formulas and patents are taken care of; it's ready for you to run right out of the gates!

2. Leverage

Leverage is by far the single most important advantage in a profession like this by allowing people to work smarter, not harder. Most people wish they had more hours in a day; however, in the same 24 hours we all have, you must work to generate income, you need to sleep, you need to be with your family or loved ones, you have to focus on your health and the list goes on with life obligations. Most people typically work eight hours a day at a job - most times, at a job they don't even like. In exchange for time, employers pay a set wage. Some employers pay employees for units of a product produced or sold - commission based and sometimes capped. Either way, employee wages will always have a ceiling.

Understand network marketing - network marketing companies pay their distributors for work done by other distributors. Similar to Bill Gates as he built his company by creating and owning a 'system'. When he sleeps he makes money, when he drives and he makes money, when he vacations he makes money. Do you think he goes into his office much? No. So by systematically increasing the number of active distributors/business builders in your downline, your income will increase, and as your system grows the number of hours you work will decrease making time for you to spend any way you wish. It is definitely well worth your time to build if you have big aspirations.

3. Passive Residual Income

You could have all the savings in the world but when that rainy day comes your savings will eventually be depleted, then where will that money come from to replace it? Network marketing is an opportunity to build an ever-increasing **passive residual income**. If people understood what residual income is they would break through brick walls to obtain it. Passive residual income is only made possible by leveraging as mentioned above. So by leveraging on other people's effort and time, a large residual income is possible because you've helped them to do the same. In this business, it's all about duplication - not just a President or CEO sitting at the very top of a company while everyone works hard while he or she benefits. It's about people helping people and when you help others to build a passive residual income you bet that you deserve the same. **You become successful only when you have helped others become successful.**

4. International Business Owner

Do you love to travel? You can literally work anywhere in the world where a network marketing company is operational. As long as you have a smartphone/laptop, WiFi and a burning desire to win, you are in business! Meet new people from all over the world with just a tap on your keyboard and see the world and experience it first-hand. I can literally choose which province, state or country I want to build in. **Truly, the world is your oyster** and keep in mind that as you decide where you want to build your business, the next benefit is key to building globally.

5. Huge Tax Perks

One of the not-so-obvious advantages of network marketing that people miss are the incredible tax perks which an 'Employee' doesn't have. When you join a network marketing company you're starting your very own home-based business and even your capital invested can be written off. For those of you who have a traditional job, you too can be earning extra income and as a huge bonus, **you will have various tax advantages over your colleagues**. If you like to travel, dine out, entertain, if you have a mortgage, car payment, fuel costs, office supplies, etc. then this is possibly the greatest advantage of all as you are allowed to deduct your expenses from your income before calculating how much tax you should pay!

I love Robert Kiyosaki's cash flow quadrant: '**Businesses earn, spend and pay taxes. Employees earn, pay taxes and spend.**' In other words, businesses spend what they earn before paying their taxes, while employees pay taxes before spending what they earn and it's usually a 30% deduction of your hard earned cash - how fair is that? Remember, with the money you save on taxes that's additional cash flow on top of the extra income you're earning with your home-based business. Consult with your local tax specialist to find out what you can deduct and have them show you how this puts you at an advantage. As someone in the business, your tax liability is not calculated on how much income you have earned. No. It's calculated based on how much of what you have earned remains after taking off some of your expenses from that income. **This is a no brainer!**

6. Time Freedom

A huge disadvantage of the traditional 9 to 5 is the lack of time freedom. When an employer trades you money for your time you are no longer free to come and go as you please; you clock in and clock out and you are at the mercy of your boss. In the cash flow quadrant, don't get Self Employed mixed up with Business Owner. Self-employed means that you now 'own' your job because if you don't work you don't get paid. Being self-employed means that there are no more 2-week paycheques, the hustle becomes real and you become a slave to your customers.

When you are a business owner, you are creating your own system and as you build your downlines in network marketing you begin to solidify your system, much like Bill Gates as mentioned before. This is a great profession for people who have children, or other obligations, where the normal hours of a 9 - 5 will not allow and keep in mind that when you work from home, or eventually on a beach, you have cut out wasted commute time. In this glorious profession, you choose with whom you wish to work with, when you want to work and best of all where you want to work, now couple that up with a leveraged residual income = **FREEDOM** to do, be and go wherever you wish, whenever you wish, never ordering from a menu based on the right hand side ever again!

7. Support

This is a people helping people kind of business. There is a famous saying in this profession, "**you're in business for yourself, but not by yourself.**" I remember being freaked out as I was stepping into the unknown with my very first try at network marketing and that statement was most comforting as I had a great mentor. As soon as you join a network marketing company, you become part of a positive and motivated team/family that has you in their best interest. It's like this, if you don't perform at a traditional job and meet your quota, or fulfil your responsibilities, you are Gonzo Alfonzo!

In network marketing, if you're not successful then your Sponsor/Up line will not be successful so it's absolutely in their best interest to help and equip you with the right tools and support that you require to become successful. Remember, it's never about you! It's all about leverage and how it can be achieved is by **supporting your people**. As you start building your own team they become your down line and you coach them into their greatness. Your team will benefit from your personal support and those of your up line and so on and so forth, you may call this 'cloning' or 'duplication'. The Company is also committed to helping you because you are their life source along with every new customer or distributor/business builder you bring and it has happened where someone found their one superstar which ended up being worth millions!

8. Personal Development

This one is my absolute favourite because when I worked corporate if I didn't take it upon myself to grow within it wouldn't happen at work and it's no wonder I left corporate, my vision became too big and clear! I was lucky to be introduced to network marketing when I was 19 years young and because of that I was exposed to a ton of personal development and as I grew within, my businesses flourished! To become a leader in this profession all network marketers are prolific readers; as the saying goes, '**leaders are readers**'. Network marketing diversifies you in skills that a traditional job doesn't focus on such as public speaking, coaching, mentoring, how to relate to others, etc. Network marketers also grow spiritually regardless of their religion because in this business it's all about your belief systems. Traditional jobs will train you and develop you just enough that you say confined to their corporate walls because why would they want you to leave when you can be building their empire while making someone else's dreams come true?

9. Training

In network marketing, you don't need any sales experience or any form of a business background. As long as you have a dream and you're coachable, and you apply what you learn to your business the network marketing vehicle is a great way to get you where you want to go faster, rather than finding a part-time job spending another 20 hours on top of your full-time 40 hour job building, yet again, someone else's empire. However, for those that are business savvy, they truly understand this type of grind and would rather grind for themselves. Training will come from corporate or different groups within the company that with different styles of training.

Again, the beauty in this business is that you get to decide whom you want to work with and whom you want as a mentor. Since all distributors are independent business owners, it is imperative that you don't 'blame' your Sponsor or Upline for your lack of success. There are many courses and a plethora of free training that can be found on the internet. As an entrepreneur, you also have to continually self-educate. Knowing your 'why' is the first step and the 'how' will follow. You must keep actively searching for training opportunities that align with you, not necessarily what is comfortable for you because as we all know, success begins outside of your comfort zone and **investing in courses and company conventions is the key to massive growth and success.**

10. Personal Branding

With all that you will learn through this profession, you may become an expert marketer, however, if trained properly you will understand that you're not a salesperson or a professional marketer for your product

or service. You are branding you and your values and what you stand for. People buy into your company or products because **they like and trust YOU**. Once you have established this for yourself, and you become a leader in your community by using your voice and helping others, your level of success is exponential and never capped.

CHAPTER EIGHT

Top Companies

Top MLM Companies in India

1. Mi Lifestyle Marketing Global Private Limited

Mi Lifestyle Marketing Global Private Limited is a direct selling company which was established in the year 2013 in Chennai. Right now it is India's one of the most popular MLM companies.

The company offers wide range of quality lifestyle products for day to day use which are approved by Ministry of AYUSH.

They offer wide range of Health and nutritional products. Go here to know more about their products.

Company's current revenue is more than Rs 1500 Crore. You can register with the company and join their wide network of distributors.

Once you have completed the registration form you need to buy their products worth Rs 1000 from their website.

That is how you become a distributor!

Initially, you can start adding 3 – 4 people as distributors under your distributor ID. Later on you can add more and see your income rise substantially.

2. Amway India

Amway is one of the oldest MLM companies operating in India. Amway is not an Indian company but it has got huge presence in India with 140 sales offices and warehouses in 34 cities.

Amway sells more than 150 personal care and health products through distributed marketing. Amway is known for its quality products especially world's No. 1 Nutrilite supplement brand.

Join as an ABO, fill the form and submit all the necessary documents. After 24 hours a new ID will be generated.

You can start selling the products to your friends and ask them to join the network. You have a great opportunity to become a business person by earning 6% to 21% of business volume depending upon monthly sale.

3. Herballife

After Amway, Herbalife is the second best US based MLM Company operating in India. The company offers some of the best nutritional supplements made out of herbs and fruits.

All of Herbalife products' are sold by its associates and are not available in any general stores.

You earn money either by selling Herbalife products to someone or sponsoring someone who sells Herbalife products. However you don't earn any money by simply recruiting or sponsoring someone.

To join the Herbalife MLM you have to pay for initial membership kit worth $60.

You can join the Herbalife and become its associate to get minimum discount of 25% on every purchase. Then you sell these products at a retail price to others. That is how you make profits.

4. Forever Living

Forever Living is another US based MLM company known for its exclusive products based on Aloe Vera.

You can find some of the best products Here!

Forever Living's MLM plan is very simple. You just have to become a FBO (Forever Business Owner) member and buy products at a wholesale price and sell them at retail price to your friends earning up to 43% in commissions.

In bonuses, you earn Group Volume Bonus up to 13% on each of the team members under you and for Leadership bonus you get 2% to 6% depending upon position in the organization.

However you don't get paid merely by recruiting people, you earn when someone sells the product.

5. Modicare

Modicare founded by Sameer Modi is one of the fastest growing Indian MLM companies in the country.

It offers wide range of products from categories like Wellness, Skin Care, Personal care, Home care etc.

What makes Modicare different from other MLM companies is their unique business plan also known as Azadi Plan.

As a Modicare consultant you can buy products 20-25% cheaper and sell it at a huge profit to others earning 25% profit. Consultants with higher sales volume are awarded Power Seller Bonus which can be between 5% – 20% depending upon BV (Business Volume).

You earn commission depending upon your level in the organization.

You also get Accumulative Performance Bonus ranging between 7% and 22%. Other bonuses are Director Bonus – 14%, Leadership Productivity Bonus – 15%.

6. RCM

RCM is one of the India's largest direct selling company with over 10 million direct selling partners spread all over the country.

Once you have become a direct seller you can start promoting RCM products and earn incentives based on purchases made by you and people in your group.

You can buy products at a 15% discount and sell at a higher MRP earning 15% to 20% in profits. You also get 10% to 32% on the purchase made by an individual in your group.

Moreover, there are different categories of bonuses like Performance Bonus, Royalty Bonus and Technical Bonus. You earn commissions between 5% and 32% depending upon your Business Volume (BV).

7. Vestige

Vestige Marketing Pvt. Ltd a direct selling company started its operation in the year 2004 offering quality health and personal care products.

Right the company has over 2000 online and offline sales outlets with 650 offices spread across India.

Vestige offers a wide range of products from health supplements to air purifier to personal care. You can download the product catalogue from here.

First you register as a Vestige Distributor and start promoting their products to people.

You earn money by not only selling products to others but also in the form of leadership bonuses, pool income and on the performance of your downline.

The Vestige business plan offers

10% – 20% Savings on Consumption

5% – 20% as Accumulative Performance Bonus

14% as a Director Bonus

15% as a Leadership Overriding Bonus

8. OriFlame

Oriflame a Swedish beauty company has a huge presence in India. OriFlame offers mainly beauty and skin care products.

However OriFlame is not a sole MLM company like RCM or Herbalife. People can buy products from their website directly and need not to buy from a direct seller.

You can register with OriFlame as a consultant and start selling products on their behalf. Once you register as a VIP customer you can buy products at a discount of 20% to 40% and sell at a higher MRP to customers.

You will earn immediate profit combined with business class benefits. Moreover, you also earn PD (Performance Discount) on achieving certain level of sales.

9. Avon

Unlike OriFlame, Avon is world's largest beauty direct seller. They are present in over 70 countries and in India they have been operating for 20 years now.

After become Avon representative you can buy their best-in-class products at a discount up to (starting from 15%) 30%, sell them to your friends and earn commission over 50%.

You can develop a team and earn more commissions on your group sales. You earn commission based on your team size and position in the organization.

On an average Avon representative in India earns Rs 20,000 to Rs 3,00,000 per month.

10. Future Maker

Hisar, Haryana based Future Maker Life Care Pvt. Limited is one of the fastest growing direct selling companies operating in India. The company is very new founded in 2015 and has grown phenomenally since then.

You can easily become a direct seller for Future Maker through an existing direct seller. There is no entry fee for registration and you also compulsory don't have to purchase any of their promotional material.

According to their business plan a direct seller gets to decide MRP that they are going to charge from their customers. So you buy products from Future Maker at a huge discount and sell at higher price to your customers.

You also get Monthly Loyalty Bonus and Weekly Team Bonus depending upon your BV (Business Volume).

They also offer you incentives depending upon number of sales each month.

11. 4Life

4Life is an US based direct selling company known for its food supplements products for general health and wellness.

4Life offers a great compensation plan for its distributors. Distributors can make a lot of money from Retail profits. As a distributor you can purchase products at a wholesale cost and resell them for a retail cost earning up to 33% profit.

You also earn 25% commission on selling certain kinds of products with higher LP (Life Points).

As a 4Life distributor you will enjoy recognition for your achievements through Rank Advancements.

You make even more if you qualify as a leader because you are eligible for Rapid Rewards. Your earn more in bonuses as you rise higher in the hierarchy from Leader through Platinum International Diamond rank.

12. DXN India

DXN a multilevel marketing company based in Malaysia but very popular in India. The company was founded by Lim Siow Jin in the year 1993.

DXN India is known for its unique products not offered by other MLM companies. The mushroom types like Ganoderma, Reishi, Lingzhi is the company's unique offering other than Food supplements, beverages and personal care products.

People join DXN as a direct seller because of remuneration given by the company.

You can earn 15% to 20% in retail profits and 6% to 21% as group bonus depending upon your sales number.

Here is the breakdown of different types of bonuses.

Start Bonus – 25% to 37%

Development Bonus – 15%

Leadership Bonus – 15%

13. NASWIZ

NASWIZ is relatively a small MLM company that offers products mainly in Home Appliance segments.

NASWIZ offers remuneration depending upon IP (Incentive Points) you earn. IP is assigned to each product you sell as a direct seller.

Following is the breakdown of their incentive structure.

● Direct Sales Incentives can be up to 30% – You buy at wholesale price and sell at a higher MRP

● Team Performance Bonus – Total accumulated IP of a direct seller depends upon IP earned by their team members.

● IP (Incentive Points) Level Bonus

● IP Leadership Bonus – 25% of total IPs generated in a given month.

14. K-Link Healthcare (India) Pvt Ltd.

K-Link a direct sales company based in Chennai was started in the year 2001.

They offer products like Health supplement, Personal Care, Beauty, Agro and FMCG. Some of their well known products are K-Liquid Chlorophyll, K-Flax, Protein Pro and Ayurveda Series.

K-Link gives 28% development bonus and 30% leadership bonus to its distributors. You also get incentives based on your business volume (BV) and position in the company.